Waste Not, Want Not

Building a Profitable Junk Removal Business

Table of Contents

Chapter 1. Introduction

In this captivating Special Report, "Waste Not, Want Not: Building a Profitable Junk Removal Business", we venture into the thriving world of junk removal - an industry that transforms "one person's trash into another's treasure". Embark on this enlightening journey, where you'll uncover the secrets of turning waste into wealth. Discover how to run a successful, profitable business removing, recycling, and repurposing items that others have discarded, thus not only saving the planet but also building a prosperous future for yourself. With an engaging blend of tried-and-tested strategies, inspiring real-life success stories, and pragmatic guidance, this comprehensive report will excite, inspire, and empower you in your entrepreneurial journey. This is an offer simply too good to refuse! Grab your copy today.

Chapter 2. Setting the Foundation: Understanding the Junk Removal Business

Understanding the junk removal business is critical to setting a solid foundation for your entrepreneurial endeavor. To successfully navigate the waters of waste removal and processing, you must familiarize yourself with the nature of the business, the dynamics of the industry, the opportunities and challenges it presents, regulatory requirements, as well as the various strategies for profitability.

2.1. The Nature of the Junk Removal Business

The junk removal business primarily involves the collection and disposal of waste materials or discarded items from homes, businesses, and construction sites. Junk removal goes beyond the regular waste collection services offered by municipal bodies. It's an industry that encompasses the collection of large, bulky items, hazardous materials, construction debris, garden waste, and electronics – essentially items that may not be catered for by regular waste management services.

The collected junk can then be disposed of through various means. These include recycling, reselling, donating to charity, or, as a last resort, disposing of in landfills. Through this process, a junk removal business contributes to waste reduction and resource conservation, fostering a better environment for all.

2.2. Industry Dynamics

The junk removal industry is a crucial part of environmental management. Its services are not only important for waste reduction but also to combat the environmental impacts of solid waste. The industry is heavily influenced by regulatory regimes, population dynamics, consumer behavior trends, and technological advancements.

The demand for junk removal services has been on the rise due to a surging population, increasing urbanization, growth in the real estate and construction industries, and changing lifestyles. Moreover, advancements in recycling technologies have opened avenues for the disposal of waste that weren't previously available.

However, like any other business, the junk removal industry faces its fair share of challenges. These include competition, regulatory hassles, and the high operational cost for waste collection and disposal.

2.3. Opportunities and Challenges

The fact that junk removal companies can have multiple revenue streams presents a fantastic business opportunity. A proactive business can take advantage of recycling, repurposing, reselling discarded items, and providing regular pick-up services to create multiple profitable business lines.

However, challenges exist. The industry is heavily regulated, requiring businesses to navigate permit acquisition, compliance, and a myriad of health and safety regulations. Moreover, the operational costs can be high, including vehicle maintenance, manpower, and waste disposal costs. The upcycle of junk is also contingent on the market for second-hand goods or recyclable materials, which fluctuates.

Despite the challenges, the increasing awareness about environmental conservation provides a ripe market for junk removal businesses, especially those that put an emphasis on recycling and responsible disposal.

2.4. Regulatory Requirements

Regulatory compliance is at the heart of a successful junk removal business. As an entrepreneur, you should familiarize yourself with all the local, state, and federal regulations that apply to waste collection, disposal, and recycling. This includes understanding the legal classifications of waste, permits, licenses, and standards for disposal and recycling.

These laws are designed to protect the environment, and non-compliance can lead to hefty penalties, legal ramifications, or license revocation. It is, therefore, crucial to ensure that your business operations are always within the ambit of the law.

2.5. Strategies for Profitability

Setting a strong business plan, pricing your services appropriately, and targeting the right markets are important steps to success. You can consider offering a range of services, from residential to commercial, to broaden your customer base. Offering eco-friendly disposal options can also distinguish your business in today's increasingly environmentally-conscious market.

Moreover, partnerships with recycling facilities and second-hand goods dealers can provide additional revenue streams. Additionally, staying updated with the latest technology and waste management trends can help increase efficiency, reduce costs, and ultimately increase profitability.

In conclusion, understanding the dynamics of the junk removal business is vital for success. With a thorough understanding of the business, you can plan effectively, navigate any hurdles, capitalize on opportunities, and build a profitable business while contributing positively to environmental conservation.

Chapter 3. Junk Removal 101: Essential Equipment and Skills You Need

Starting a junk removal business may seem like a straightforward endeavor - after all, how complicated can trash be? But if you delve beneath the surface, you'll discover that achieving success in this industry is no less challenging, rewarding, or complex as any other. The first step begins with equipping yourself physically as well as intellectually. This chapter unravels what essential tools, equipment, and skills you need to hit the ground running.

3.1. Tools of the Trade: Essential Physical Equipment

Your tools are your battlefield allies. With the right combination, you can tackle any job, big or small, swiftly and efficiently.

1. A Reliable Junk Removal Vehicle

At the heart of any junk removal operation is a sturdy, reliable vehicle. A truck or van is your lifeline, enabling you to transport junk from customer locations to disposal or recycling centers. Choose a vehicle with a sizable cargo space, easy maneuverability, and excellent fuel efficiency. Look for models that have long lifespans and low maintenance costs to keep your operational expenses lean.

1. Personal Protective Equipment (PPE)

Safety isn't negotiable. When dealing with junk, you'll encounter all kinds of materials and objects. Protective equipment—including gloves, steel-toe boots, safety goggles, and heavy-duty clothing—protects you from potential injuries. Regularly inspect and replace worn-out PPE.

1. Simple Hand Tools

A junk removal job often involves more than just picking up trash. You may need to dismantle large pieces of furniture, remove built-in cabinets, or tear up old carpeting. Having basic hand tools, such as hammers, wrenches, screwdrivers, and pliers can be a lifesaver.

1. Heavy Equipment

For larger, more complex tasks, you might need heavy-duty equipment such as dollies, sturdy ropes, hand trucks, or even a Bobcat. Owning or renting such equipment can significantly expand your service capabilities.

3.2. Mastering Software: Embracing Digitalization

Just as essential as your physical tools is your adeptness with digital technology. The right software can streamline your business operations, making you more efficient and effective.

1. Route Planning Software

This software can save you tons of time by planning your pick-ups and drop-offs in the most efficient way possible, reducing fuel consumption and increasing the amount of work you can accomplish in a day.

1. Customer Relationship Management (CRM) Software

CRM software allows you to manage client information, keep track of requests, streamline your billing process, and provide top-tier customer service consistently.

1. Waste Tracking Software

With regulations around waste disposal tightening, a waste tracking software can ensure you're compliant, avoiding potential costly fines and penalties.

3.3. Essential Soft Skills

Having the right equipment and software is only part of the equation. The other half hinges upon your soft skills that can really set apart your junk removal business from others.

1. Customer Service

Providing exceptional customer service is a crucial part of running a successful junk removal business. A happy customer is a repeat customer and often a source of valuable referrals. Be punctual, respectful, clean, and efficient. Listen to your customers and strive to exceed their expectations.

1. Entrepreneurial Skills

Entrepreneurial skills such as decision-making, problem-solving, strategic planning, and continuously seeking out new opportunities are vital to the growth and sustainability of your business. As you gain experience in the industry, you'll need to make critical decisions that will shape your business's direction and future.

1. Environmental Literacy

A good understanding of ecology and environmental regulations will serve your business well. Not only will you be compliant with relevant laws, but you can portray your business as actively working towards a greener planet, which is a significant selling point for many clients.

1. Negotiation Skills

You'll often find yourself dealing with a variety of individuals and businesses - from customers and employees to waste management facilities and recycling centers. Efficient negotiation skills can help you secure favorable terms and agreements.

1. Team Building

As your business grows, you'll likely need to hire employees. Your ability to build a strong, motivated team will play an integral role in your success. Choose people who are dedicated, hard-working, and believe in your vision.

3.4. The Learning Curve: Continuous Improvement

In the junk removal business, there is always something to learn, from new waste management practices and emerging recycling technologies to changes in local, state, and national regulations. Embracing continuous learning and improvement can enable you to adapt to changing conditions and stay ahead of your competition.

Congratulations! Now you have a holistic overview of the essential equipment and skills required to start a junk removal business. In the next chapter, we'll dive into how to create an effective business plan that puts you on the path to success.

Chapter 4. Mastering the Economics: Pricing Strategies for Profitability

The concept of pricing is both an art and science. Understanding the dynamics involved is vital to the profitability of any junk removal operation.

4.1. Understanding Your Costs

To effectively price your services, you must first comprehend your business's costs. These include the obvious overheads, such as vehicle expenses (fuel, insurance, maintenance, etc.) and labor, as well as the less-evident ones like office space, marketing, and insurance. Understanding these costs is the foundation on which friendly pricing begins.

Your cost structure will impact your pricing model. Therefore a review of the costs associated with delivering your service will give you a baseline to help determine what your pricing options might look like. You need to factor in the current expenses associated with running your business. These could be fuel costs, landfill fees, staff wages, and the price of your operating licenses, among others.

4.2. The Optimal Pricing Model

When it is about pricing your junk removal services, two principal models can be considered – Flat rate and Value-based pricing.

Flat Rate Pricing: This is a pricing strategy where you charge a single fixed fee for a service, regardless of usage or amount of junk removed. Flat-rate pricing can be a safe bet, appealing to clients as it lets them know in advance what the service will cost.

Value-Based Pricing: Value-based pricing, on the other hand, prices your service according to the perceived value to the customer rather than according to the actual cost of the service provided. The added value you provide could be in the form of convenience, time saving, or eco-friendly disposal methods.

Deciding between these two approaches to pricing will depend largely on your business's unique circumstances, including your operational costs and the competitive landscape in your market.

4.3. To Discount or Not to Discount

In the world of junk removal services, offering discounts can be a powerful tool to attract new customers or incentivize repeat business. However, you must be strategic with your discounts. Offering too many discounts or pricing services too low can diminish perceived value, while rarely offering discounts may allow your competitors to appear more affordable.

When offering a discount, make sure you're still covering your costs and making a profit. If you're using discounts as a means to attract new customers, also have a plan to retain them once the discounted rate expires.

4.4. Competitor Pricing Analysis

Knowing your competition's charges and how you stack up against them is vital. It is as important as knowing your costs. Benchmarking your pricing against competitors gives you an idea of what customers are willing to pay for your services and where you can leverage your unique value propositions for competitive advantage.

It's not always about being the cheapest. Competitor pricing analysis can reveal opportunities to justify higher prices based on the unique value you provide, such as superior service, quicker turnaround times, or more eco-friendly disposal processes.

4.5. Strategic Experimentation

No one pricing model will be the perfect fit. Once you've chosen a strategy, don't be afraid to experiment with adjustments and monitor the results. Just ensure you're doing so in a controlled, measurable environment, so you can accurately evaluate how changes are impacting your bottom line. Strategic experimentation, backed by informed data, is a healthy approach to honing in on the most profitable pricing strategy for your business.

Your pricing should never be set in stone. The markets evolve, new competitors enter, economic situations change, and so do your costs and your customers' perceptions of value. A periodic review and adjustment of your pricing will not only resonate better with your clients but also ensure that you are consistently optimizing your profitability.

4.6. Conclusion

Pricing is a powerful driver of profitability for any business. However, precise and strategic pricing is particularly essential in a junk removal business, where costs can fluctuate and the perceived value delivered to the customer can dramatically influence what they're willing to pay for the service.

By effectively understanding your costs, evaluating your pricing model, leveraging strategic discounts, conducting competitor pricing analysis, and wisely experimenting, you can master the economics of pricing in your junk removal business. This will result not only in enhanced profitability but in a more sustainable and successful business over the long term. The journey through these pricing strategies can be just as rewarding as the ultimate destination of increased profit margins.

Chapter 5. Marketing Magic: Attracting and Retaining Customers

In today's hyper-competitive marketplace, attracting and retaining customers is paramount to success, particularly in the junk removal business, where sustaining a continual flow of clients can be challenging. By embracing an innovative marketing strategy and fostering a culture focused on customer satisfaction, your junk removal business can flourish.

5.1. The Power of a Unique Value Proposition

At the cornerstone of an effective marketing strategy is your Unique Value Proposition (UVP), which not only differentiates your business from competitors but also and more importantly, tells prospective clients why they should choose your service over another. A powerful UVP reduces price-sensitivity, attracts quality leads and eventually turns them into loyal customers.

Your UVP should quickly communicate the following key components: . What service or product your junk removal business provides . Who your target market is, and why your service is specially catered for them . How your business is uniquely capable of meeting their needs

Keep your UVP succinct, clear, and compelling—a phrase or sentence that anyone can understand should be your goal.

5.2. Brand Building: An Essential Investment

Branding isn't just about logos and taglines—it's about creating an identity that your customers can relate to. Making an emotional connection with your customers is what makes them remember you and choose you over competitors.

Consider these three elements when developing your brand: . Personality: What tone or style will you use to communicate with clients? . Promise: What consistent value can customers expect to see from your business? . Positioning: How do you differentiate from competitors in delivering that value?

Ensure that every aspect of your business—from your website and social media accounts to your team's uniforms and truck designs—reflect who you are as a brand.

5.3. Utilizing Digital Marketing

The advent of digital technology has dramatically transformed the business landscape. A strong online presence is no longer optional; it's a necessity.

Two key areas are Search Engine Optimization (SEO) and Social Media. SEO allows your business to appear at the top of search engine results when a user inputs relevant keywords, increasing your visibility. Social media platforms like Facebook, Instagram, and LinkedIn enables you to build your brand, engage with potential customers, and showcase your services.

Don't forget email marketing, another powerful tool that, when used effectively, can greatly increase customer retention rates. Collect emails from your customers and ensure you send them valuable information regularly.

5.4. Traditional Marketing Still Holds Value

Despite the digital age, traditional marketing methods still hold value. Think direct mail, print advertising, trade shows, or networking events. Networking with real estate agents, property managers, and home improvement companies is a lucrative way to get new business, as they often require junk removal services.

5.5. Customer Retention: It's Easier to Keep than to get New Customers

Once you've obtained a client, your work has just begun. Keeping customers is just as essential as finding new ones, if not more so.

Two key strategies to customer retention are providing exceptional customer service and setting up a customer loyalty program. Ensure your team always delivers top-notch service, and that any customer issues are handled swiftly and professionally. Meanwhile, a customer loyalty program could involve discounts on future junk removal or even a referral program where clients receive bonuses for referring your business to others.

Remember, satisfied customers are your best advertisement. Word-of-mouth marketing from a pleased client can bring in more business than even the most successful paid marketing campaign.

In conclusion, marketing your junk removal business requires a multifaceted approach comprising of a clearly defined UVP, a solid brand, and a blend of digital and traditional marketing methods. Most importantly, it entails providing a service that keeps customers coming back. Practice these strategies, and your junk removal business will not only survive but thrive, even in the most competitive of markets.

Chapter 6. Go Green: Embracing Sustainability in Junk Removal

Sustainability isn't just a buzzword; in fact, it's much more than that. It's the need of the hour and a crucial factor to consider when running any business in the modern era, including a junk removal one. As the consciousness about environmental issues related to waste disposal grows, enterprises that follow eco-friendly practices gain a competitive edge.

6.1. Consider the Environmental Impact

When it comes to junk removal, we must consider the environmental impact. Not everything we discard ends up in landfill sites. A significant portion winds up littering our landscapes, water bodies, and more. Much of it is non-biodegradable and remains in the environment for hundreds of years, polluting ecosystems and damaging biodiversity.

To combat this, we must strive for responsible waste disposal and management. Junk removal businesses should aim to cut down the amount of waste that ends up in landfills and instead, focus on recycling, salvage, and re-purposing.

6.2. The 3 R's: Reduce, Reuse, Recycle

In keeping your business green, remember the 3 R's - Reduce, Reuse, Recycle. Let's delve deeper into each of these concepts:

6.3. The Profit Potential of Sustainability

Recycle: Make sure that recyclable items do not end up in the trash. Segregate recyclable materials and channel them to appropriate recycling facilities.

Adopting environmentally friendly practices can also significantly enrich the profitability of your junk removal business besides protecting the environment. Selling reclaimed items, for instance, can provide an extra stream of revenue.

Moreover, a sustainable business resonates well with the customers of today who are more conscious about their environmental footprint. Having a visible commitment to the environment can fortify your brand image, setting you apart from competitors.

6.4. Partnerships and Certifications

Forming alliances with recycling facilities and green organizations can boost your business's credibility. Some alliances may even offer exclusive access to resources, shared marketing efforts, and communal benefits.

Additionally, acquiring green certifications such as LEED (Leadership in Energy and Environmental Design) can help to enhance your business image and attract more customers. These certifications confer to potential customers that your business is committed to the principles of green operation and offers environmentally-friendly services.

6.5. Educate Your Customers

Education plays a pivotal role in creating a sustainable business. Customers often lack awareness about the correct methods of disposal and the different recyclable materials.

Organize workshops, create informational content on your website, and use your social media platforms to educate your clients about correct waste disposal. Guide them about waste segregation and explain how small behavioral changes can contribute enormously towards protecting the environment.

6.6. Embrace Technological Innovations

Technology can be a valuable ally in your green endeavors. By implementing waste management software, you can optimize routes for pickup and drop-off, reducing carbon emissions.

Moreover, consider investing in hybrid or electric vehicles for operations. While the upfront costs might be higher, the long-term savings on fuel, coupled with the low environmental impact, represent a significant benefit.

In conclusion, running a sustainable junk removal business is not just about doing good for the environment. It's also a sound financial strategy that can differentiate your brand, attract more customers, and open new revenue streams. For this transition, you will need to focus on education, partnership, and the innovative use of technology.

Chapter 7. Understanding Regulations: Keeping Your Business Lawful

Understanding the regulations is an essential part of operating a profitable junk removal business. Equipping oneself with ample understanding of the applicable laws will save you from potential legal troubles, fines, and a tarnished reputation. It will also show your clients that you're a serious professional who takes the job and the planet's welfare to heart.

7.1. Know Your Federal Regulations

At the national level in the U.S., the Environmental Protection Agency (EPA) is the governing body responsible for the management of waste removal and disposal. The agency's guidelines, attached to regulations like the Resource Conservation and Recovery Act(RCRA), guide how you should handle solid and hazardous wastes.

The RCRA outlines the "cradle to grave" system that requires businesses to track their harmful waste from creation to disposal. It also delineates the types of trash that are considered harmful.

As a business owner, familiarize yourself with the rules and regulations contained in the RCRA and regularly check for updates on the EPA's website. Ensuring that your operations align with the law will protect your company and reduce the risk of costly legal complications.

7.2. Understand State and Local Ordinances

Laws and regulations can vary wildly from one location to another, so it's crucial that you understand the state and local ordinances you'll be working within. Start by researching your local health department and city or county government websites for relevant information, as many have specific junk removal regulations.

In many states, for example, it's a requirement to separate recyclable materials from the rest of the waste. Failure to do so could result in significant fines. Some areas might also have rules about the disposal of certain items, like electronics or appliances.

Some cities or counties require permits or licenses for specific kinds of debris removal, especially when dealing with potentially hazardous materials. Ensure you obtain, maintain, and regularly renew these documents to avoid legal issues and interruptions in your operations.

7.3. Handling Hazardous Waste

When it comes to junk removal, not all waste is created equal. Certain types such as batteries, pesticides, paints, cleaners, oils, refrigerants, and other chemicals are considered hazardous.

The EPA defines hazardous waste by four characteristics: ignitability, corrosivity, reactivity, and toxicity. Each has specific handling and disposal requirements, often more stringent than regular waste. Improper disposal could potentially harm the environment and human health, thus facing hefty penalties.

You must be trained and educated on how to handle hazardous waste correctly. The Occupational Safety and Health Administration (OSHA) offers training that can be beneficial in this regard. Also, be aware that licensing and special permissions might be required for certain types of hazardous waste.

Understanding hazardous waste is a crucial part of being a responsible junk removal business owner. It ensures that you not only comply with regulations but also protect your employees, customers, and the environment.

7.4. Occupational Health and Safety

The junk removal business is not devoid of health and safety risks. Workers risk exposure to harmful substances, physical injuries, or diseases from sharp objects and unhygienic conditions. This calls for an understanding of the Occupational Safety and Health Act (OSHA), which sets out guidelines for the safety and health of your employees.

OSHA requires providing workers with suitable protective gear and adequately training them to handle a variety of wastes safely. Regular training sessions and safety drills, providing first aid kits, and ensuring cleanliness can all help reduce the risk of workplace injuries and subsequent litigation.

Personal protection equipment such as gloves, boots, goggles, and masks are a must, and their usage should be enforced strictly. The business may also need insurance to cover possible injuries or accidents.

7.5. Disposal and Recycling Regulations

Proper disposal of waste is a key aspect of junk removal business. However, adopting recycling can further boost your credibility and profit margins. More than just moral and environmental imperatives, recycling regulations have become more stringent, with many states demanding that certain waste types be recycled.

Ensure that your business disposes of waste at licensed facilities, knowing the local dumpsites, and adhering to their regulations. Being aware of recycling centers specializing in tires, electronics, metals, textiles, etc can further increase your revenue, as certain recyclable items can be sold for a fee.

Your business could face significant penalties if not disposing of waste responsibly. Keeping abreast of the up-to-date practices of disposal in your jurisdiction is a fundamental responsibility.

Navigating the complex landscape of regulations is a necessary element in starting and maintaining a successful junk removal business. Do your research and stay informed about changes in the law or industry practices to ensure you're always in compliance and protect your business, your employees, and your clients while also protecting the environment. Being lawful isn't just about avoiding penalties - it's also about building a reputation as a dependable and responsible business that customers can trust. This level of trust can translate into repeat business, referrals, and a long-term, profitable future for your company.

Chapter 8. Scaling Up: Expanding Your Junk Removal Business

The decision to scale up a business, any business, requires careful consideration and strategic planning. Businesses at every scale have their unique challenges, but the joy of scaling up is the act of turning a small venture into a robust, revenue-making entity. Of particular importance in a junk removal business, embracing growth means expanding your reach, serving more customers, and ultimately, rescuing more items from the landfills.

8.1. Understanding When to Scale Up

First, it's important to recognize when scaling up is the appropriate next step. Businesses scale up when they've already proven to be successful and are ready to take on more. If you're finding yourself turning away business because you're too busy, it might be time to expand. Or perhaps you've noticed that you're outgrowing your workspace. Maybe you have a sizeable cash reserve on hand that you're ready to reinvest back into your business. All of these are great indicators that it's time to consider scaling up your junk removal business.

Remember, every business is unique. Scaling could mean investing in more and larger trucks, hiring more crews, or expanding operations into new neighborhoods or cities. What scaling looks like for your business will depend greatly on where you currently are and where you want to be.

8.2. Investing in Equipment and Manpower

You can't show up to collect junk without the proper equipment. As your business grows and evolves, you'll likely need to invest in additional or different types of tools and vehicles. The kind of equipment will depend on the services you're providing and the local market conditions. Saying 'yes' to jobs that were once unmanageable is now possible with the right equipment.

Similarly, growing your business will inevitably necessitate hiring more staffers or contractors. Recruitment and training are two crucial areas to focus on. Though these both can be time-consuming and costly endeavors, it's worth investing in finding the right people from the offset.

8.3. Diversifying Your Services

As your business grows, it's important to note that growth can often come from diversifying. You could decide to expand the type of junk you remove. You might selectively sort through the items and sell valuable ones instead of sending them all to be recycled.

Businesses can also diversify by offering related services. For example, some garbage removal companies have added cleaning services, education on waste management, waste analysis, or recycling advice to their offerings. This not only provides an additional revenue stream but also increases your business's allure by providing more comprehensive services.

8.4. Expanding Your Territory

Expanding into new neighborhoods or cities is a strategy many businesses utilize when scaling up. Remember that as you grow, you'll need to understand the demographics of your expansion areas, including customer trends and needs, local recycling facilities' capacities, and competition.

It might be beneficial to pursue partnerships with local organizations or businesses in your new territory. These relationships can help you access new clientele, build a positive reputation in the community, and learn about local waste management systems.

8.5. Keeping Your Finances in Check

While it's exciting to think about scaling up, it's important to keep a hold on your financial situation. As your business grows, so do the risks. Budget your expenses carefully and always keep a close eye on your cash flow.

Remember that growing your business will mean tackling more substantial jobs, often requiring taking risks. It would help if you were prepared for this inevitable part of entrepreneurship. Always have a contingency plan, and ensure that you're not stretching yourself or your resources too thin.

8.6. Embracing Technology

Consider upgrading your technology as you scale your business. Digitizing your processes will streamline your operations, making them more efficient. Automated scheduling, state-of-the-art sorting equipment, and even customer relationship management (CRM) software can all dramatically improve your day-to-day operations.

In an increasingly digital age, your online presence is crucial too. Consider investing in building a robust website with online booking capabilities and a social media presence to market your services.

8.7. Conclusion

Scaling up your junk removal business can be a rewarding journey that takes you from a startup to a thriving enterprise. However, it's crucial you take decisive and informed steps towards growth. Highlight your strengths, address your weaknesses, and maintain a clear vision as you navigate this exciting phase of your business journey.

Never lose sight of your core mission - you're not just running a business; you're saving the planet one piece of trash at a time. It's these rich core values that will anchor you during the hectic business growth periods.

Finally, note that scaling a business is not a one-time event – it's a series of incremental steps. As you continue to grow, keep learning, refining your processes, tweaking your job efficiencies, and focusing on customers' needs. It's only then you'll truly transform from a modest junk removal venture into a mighty empire, one that not only profits but also contributes to a more sustainable world.

Chapter 9. Building a Team: Hiring Strategies for Growth

Starting your own junk removal business can be an exciting venture, but it takes more than just a truck and a love of scavenging to transform waste into wealth. To truly grow and scale your business, you will need to build a dedicated and committed team. In this crucial part of your business journey, hiring strategies are essential.

9.1. Initial Recruitment Strategies

The initial hiring process is one of the most essential steps in building your junk removal team. It forms the foundation of your workforce and sets the stage for how your business will grow. Identifying the right candidates requires a clear understanding of the job requirements and responsibilities.

Begin by crafting a detailed job description for the junk removal employees. This job description should outline the integral tasks of the job like customer interaction, loading and unloading items, identifying recyclable materials, and basic driving requirements. In addition to job details, be sure to highlight any necessary skills, like physical fitness and a good attitude.

Once the job description is solidified, you can tap into a broad range of channels to reach out to potential candidates. Traditional job boards, online recruitment websites, social media, and local community postings are all viable options. Make sure to leverage your personal network too, as referrals can often result in exceptional hires.

9.2. Interviewing and Selection

Your application and resume screening process should be rigorous, focusing more on skills, previous experience, and attitude. Given the physical nature of the job, you may choose to use physical assessments as part of the screening process.

Remember, the interview is not just about evaluating the candidate's skills and experiences; it's also the right time to gauge their commitment, attitude, and whether they fit into your company culture. Don't overlook the importance of soft skills such as customer relations, time management, and initiative, which are vital in the junk removal industry.

9.3. Training Onboard

The training process is crucial, as it ensures that your newly hired employees are equipped to perform their tasks efficiently. This training should include physical training to handle heavy loads, procedural training for waste handling and disposal, and customer service training.

Safety should be a top-of-mind concern in the junk removal business. So don't skimp on safety training. Ensure they understand all the safety protocols, including proper lifting techniques, personal protective equipment (PPE) usage, and emergency procedures.

9.4. Building a Culture of Growth

Fostering a positive and motivating company culture is fundamental. This can help boost employee morale, reduce turnover, and increase productivity. Achieving this involves open communication, regular performance feedback, providing opportunities for growth, and creating a team-oriented environment.

Consider implementing incentive schemes for referrals, customer satisfaction, or reaching recycling goals. Annual team-building exercises and regular employee recognition can also go a long way in enriching your company culture.

9.5. Continuous Recruitment and Team Expansion

Continuous recruitment is an effective strategy for consistent growth. This entails a constant search for potential hires and keeping a talent pool ready. Creating intern opportunities or part-time positions can be a fantastic way for continuous recruitment and can provide a reliable stream of candidates.

Team expansion is unavoidable as your business grows. The key to successful expansion lies in thorough planning, understanding capacity, and not overstretching resources. When adding to your team, ensure that you can maintain quality standards and effectively manage the increasing workload.

In conclusion, building a team for your junk removal business requires a well-defined recruitment strategy, proper interviewing and selection practices, thorough, safety-focused training, and fostering a growth-oriented company culture. By adhering to these steps, you will establish a robust team foundation that can sustain your business growth, drive profits, and keep you at the forefront of the junk removal industry.

Chapter 10. Financial Management: Budgeting and Revenue Optimization

Understanding your financial position and learning how to manage your money effectively is a key factor in the success of any business. Good financial management involves being able to balance short and long-term goals and having the necessary tools and information to make the right decisions.

10.1. Budgeting in a Junk Removal Business

Budgeting is one of the most crucial aspects of financial management. It involves establishing both short- and long-term objectives, identifying sources of income and expenditure, and creating a plan to ensure that your junk removal business remains financially viable.

There are two primary types of budgets you'll prepare for your business: the operating budget and the capital budget. The operating budget focuses on the income and expenses related to day-to-day business operations. These might include costs such as fuel for your vehicles, employees' wages, and disposal fees. On the other hand, the capital budget includes long-term investments for the future growth of your business like vehicles, equipment, real estate, and more.

Create a monthly operating budget by listing all your expected income and expenditure. To calculate your anticipated revenue, consider the kinds of junk removal services you'll offer – residential, commercial, or event clean-ups – and how many clients you can reasonably expect to service within a month. Be sure to factor in seasonality - certain periods, like the spring cleaning season or holidays, may bring more work.

Your operating expenses might include salaries, truck maintenance, fuel, disposal fees, and insurance. Allocate a certain proportion of your income for these expenditures. Also, consider "contingency" costs or unexpected expenses, such as equipment repairs.

A capital budget is important when scaling your business. Assess your long-term needs, such as bigger trucks, more employees, or expanded services. These investment decisions should be guided by a careful cost-benefit analysis to understand the potential return on each investment.

10.2. Revenue Optimization

Revenue optimization involves strategies that allow you to maximize your income while keeping costs low – crucial for the profitability of your junk removal business.

One efficient strategy is to diversify your service offering. For instance, instead of offering only pure junk removal, consider adding recycling and repurposing services. This could mean separating recyclable junk from non-recyclable, selling reusable items, or offering to transport items for donation.

Another effective way to optimize revenue is to implement a dynamic pricing model. Adjust your prices based on demand, taking into account factors such as the quantity of junk, difficulty of removal, or location. High demand periods may allow for higher prices.

Strategic partnerships also present an opportunity for revenue optimization. Collaborate with local recycling centers, second-hand stores, or charitable organizations, as these may have financial benefits.

Offering exceptional customer service can encourage repeat business and referrals, ancillary revenue sources that can significantly bolster your bottom line.

You could also explore overnight services or priority services for a premium charge. Such add-ons can enhance client loyalty and encourage higher spending.

10.3. The Role of Financial Software

Accounting software can simplify financial management for your junk removal business. It can assist with the creation and management of budgets, tax preparation, monitoring invoices and payments, and generating financial reports with ease.

Many modern software solutions also have robust analytics capabilities. By collecting and analyzing your financial data, they can help you identify trends and patterns, making your business decisions more informed. These insights can assist you in recognizing profitable service areas, optimizing pricing, and understanding peak work seasons.

In conclusion, financial management via careful budgeting and strategic revenue optimization is essential to the success of a junk removal business. Understanding and controlling your expenses while implementing strategies for revenue growth can put your business in a position for sustained profitability.

Chapter 11. Staying Ahead: Innovations and Trends in Junk Removal

While it may be a humble beginning, garage sales and flea markets have been and will always be the classic goldmines - where you might just find an invaluable antique between the endless piles of discarded items. However, to stay competitive in the lucrative junk removal industry, you need to constantly innovate and keep up with evolving trends. This chapter will delve into key innovations and trends that can significantly influence your junk removal business's profitability and sustainability.

11.1. Innovation One: Technological Advancements

In today's world, if you're not tech-savvy, you're already lagging. The influx of technology into every aspect of entrepreneurship is inevitable, and the junk removal business is no exception. Companies are leveraging digital platforms for online booking, route optimization, and customer satisfaction tracking.

We'll look into some of these below.

- **Online Booking and Scheduling**: Having an online platform where customers can book and schedule removals not only increases convenience but also efficiency. This automated approach eliminates tedious paperwork, reduces human error, and ensures a seamless customer experience. Websites or mobile apps with robust user interfaces and clear communication channels are essential tech-tools.

- **Route Optimization Software**: In the junk removal business, time is money. The more pickups and deliveries you can perform in a day, the more profit you make. That's where Route Optimization Software comes in. It uses sophisticated algorithms to provide the most efficient routes, saving time and reducing fuel costs.

- **Customer Satisfaction Tracking**: This tool helps you measure and monitor your service quality. It involves collecting online reviews, ratings, and customer feedback, enabling businesses to directly address customers' needs and concerns, hence boosting loyalty and retention.

11.2. Innovation Two: Eco-Friendly Practices

The junk removal industry is being reshaped by the green revolution with an increasing focus on sustainable and eco-friendly practices.

- **Reuse and Resale**: By identifying items that still have life left in them and finding ways to reuse or resell, junk removal businesses can enhance profitability while also positively impacting the environment.

- **Recycling**: With the increasing waste crisis, recycling efforts are gaining prominence. Sorting out recyclables from the collected junk and selling them to recycling facilities can add a significant revenue stream to your business.

- **Composting**: Organic waste like food scraps and yard waste forms a substantial portion of the junk collected. By composting this waste, businesses can generate a sellable product – compost, which has a high demand in agriculture and gardening.

11.3. Innovation Three: Niche Services

While general junk removal will always be needed, there is a vast array of niche services that you can offer.

- **E-waste Removal**: With a surge in electronic use, e-waste has become a significant global problem. Offering specialized e-waste removal services can set your business apart.

- **Construction Debris Removal**: Get in touch with construction companies and offer them debris removal services. Steel, wood, and concrete can fetch a good price in the resale market.

- **Hazardous Waste Removal**: Hazardous waste needs special handling. By training your team to handle and remove hazardous waste safely, you can tap into this niche market.

- **Hoarding Help**: Hoarding is a serious issue that affects several people. By offering specialized clean-up services, you can quite literally change lives.

11.4. Trends in the Industry

Staying on top of industry trends is intrinsically associated with being competitive in the market. Here are some notable trends:

- **Franchising**: As the demand in junk removal grows, so does the opportunity for franchising. This enables a faster and more structured route to business expansion.

- **Charitable Partnerships**: A rising trend is partnering with local charities, turning donatable items into an opportunity to give back to the community. Businesses get the dual benefit of decluttering and helping those in need.

- **DIY Junk Removal**: The rise of minimalism has made DIY junk removal popular. Companies now offer rental dumpster services targeting this market.

- **Corporate Contracts**: More companies are prioritizing sustainability, creating opportunities for junk removal firms to secure long-term corporate contracts.

Navigating through this sea of innovations and trends can seem overwhelming. But, by keeping your eyes open, continually educating yourself, and being ready to adapt, you can ensure your junk removal business is not just surviving, but thriving. Remember, it's not the strongest that survives; it's those most adaptable to change. Navigate these changes wisely, and your journey from waste to wealth will be both prosperous and fulfilling.